T0044826

ANDRÉ PREVIN

THREE DICKINSON SONGS

for Soprano and Piano

ED 4113

First printing: March 2000

ISBN 0-634-00662-2

G. SCHIRMER, Inc.

DISTRIBUTED BY

HAL•LEONARD®
CORPORATION

7777 W. BLUEMOUND RD. P.O. BOX 13819 MILWAUKEE, WI 53213

The Three Dickinson Songs *were written for Renée Fleming,*
who gave the first performance with Richard Bado, piano,
on December 18, 1999 at Louis Frechette Hall, Quebec

duration: ca. 10 minutes

1. As Imperceptibly as Grief

As imperceptibly as Grief
The summer lapsed away—
Too imperceptible at last
To seem like Perfidy—

A Quietness distilled
As Twilight long begun,
Or Nature spending with herself
Sequestered Afternoon—

The Dusk drew earlier in—
The Morning foreign shone—
A courteous, yet harrowing Grace,
As Guest, that would be gone—

And thus, without a Wing
Or service of a Keel
Our Summer made her light escape
Into the Beautiful.

2. Will There Really Be a Morning?

Will there really be a "Morning"?
Is there such a thing as "Day"?
Could I see it from the mountains
If I were as tall as they?

Has it feet like water lilies?
Has it feathers like a bird?
Is it brought from famous countries
Of which I have never heard?

Oh some scholar! Oh some sailor!
Oh some wise man from the skies!
Please to tell a little pilgrim
Where the place called "Morning" lies!

3. Good Morning Midnight

Good morning midnight,
I'm coming home.
Day got tired of me.
How could I of him?

Sunshine was a sweet place.
I liked to stay—
But morn didn't want me now,
So good night day!

I can look, can't I,
When the East is red?
The hills have a way then
That puts the heart abroad.

You are not so fair, midnight.
I chose day—
But please take a little girl
He turned away!

for Renée Fleming

THREE DICKINSON SONGS

1. As Imperceptibly as Grief

Emily Dickinson

André Previn

Copyright © 1999 by G. Schirmer, Inc. (ASCAP), New York, NY
All Rights Reserved. International Copyright Secured.
Warning: Unauthorized reproduction of this publication is
prohibited by Federal law and subject to criminal prosecution.

Na-ture spend-ing with her-self   Se - ques-tered Af-ter-noon—

The Dusk drew ear-lier in—   The   Morn - ing for - eign   shone—   A

cour - te - ous,   yet   har-row-ing Grace,   As   Guest, that   would   be

gone— And thus, with - out a Wing

Or ser-vice of a Keel Our Sum-mer made her light es-cape

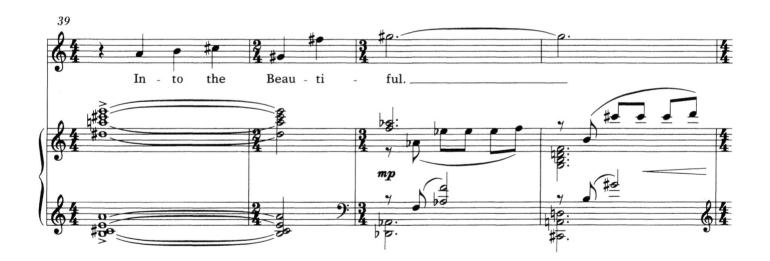

In - to the Beau - ti - ful.

moving ahead

2. Will There Really Be a Morning?

Very fast ♩ = ca. 136

Will there _ real - ly be _ a

"Morn-ing"? Is there _ such a thing _ as "Day"?

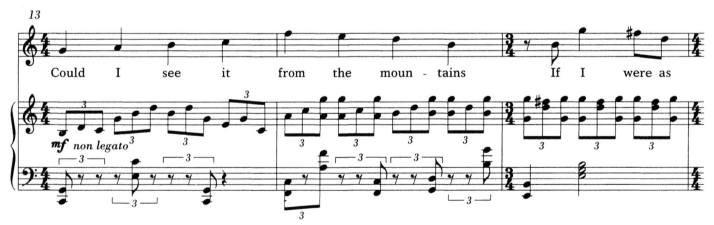

Could I see it from the moun - tains If I were as

tall as they?

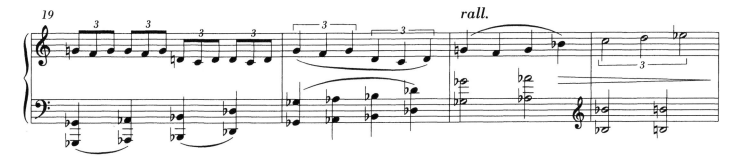

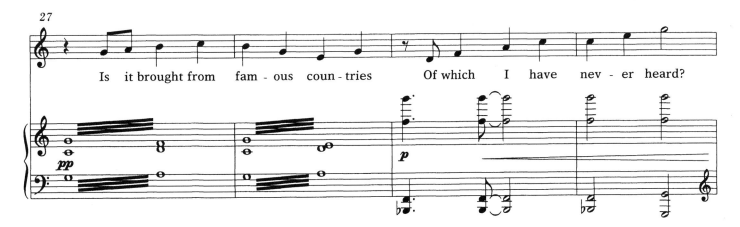

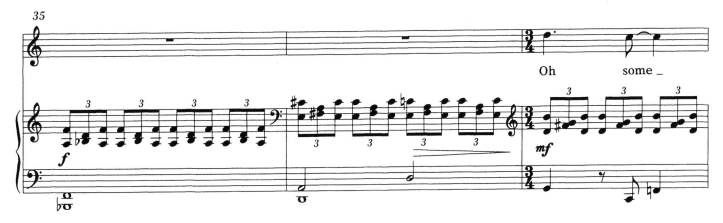

schol - ar! __ Oh some sail - or! Oh some _

wise man __ from the skies! Please to __

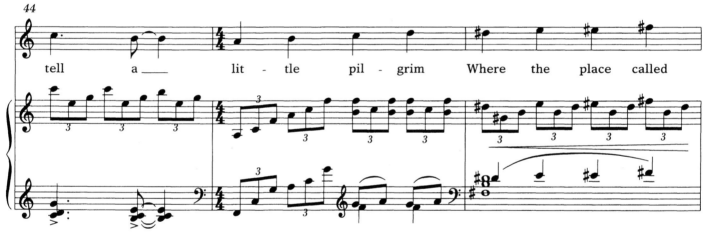

tell a __ lit - tle pil - grim Where the place called

"Morn - ing" lies! __

3. Good Morning Midnight